WREATHS
'round the year

Photography: Evan Bracken
Editorial Assistance: Carol Taylor
Design: Rob Pulleyn, Dawn Cusick
Production: Judy Clark
Typesetting: Elaine Thompson

To Tim, whose *joie de vivre* offers everlasting inspiration.

ISBN 0-8069-7468-0 Softback
ISBN 0-8069-7469-9 Hardback

10 9 8 7 6 5 4 3 2

A Sterling/Lark Book

Produced by Altamont Press, Inc.
50 College Street, Asheville, NC 28801, USA

Published in 1990 by Sterling Publishing Co., Inc.
387 Park Avenue South, New York, NY 10016

© 1990, Altamont Press

Distributed in Canada by Sterling Publishing
c/o Canadian Manda Group, P.O. Box 920, Station U
Toronto, Ontario, Canada M8Z 5P9
Distributed in the United Kingdom by Cassell PLC
Villiers House, 41/47 Strand, London WC2N 5JE, England
Distributed in Australia by Capricorn, Ltd.,
P.O. Box 665, Lane Cove, NSW 2066

WREATHS
'round the year

Dawn Cusick & Rob Pulleyn

A Sterling/Lark Book
Sterling Publishing Co., Inc.   New York

Contents

Introduction

Since the early Greeks first made wreaths of laurel branches to recognize the athletic achievements of their citizens, wreaths have held an elusive attraction for human-kind. As adornments for the front door, they send out greetings of welcome and symbolize good will. As indoor decorations, they celebrate the colors and joys of special holidays throughout the year. And as a craft, wreathmaking has something to offer just about everyone.

Most wreaths are simple to make, requiring little time or monetary investment and providing years of enjoyment. By the time you've finished reading through the following chapter on wreathmaking basics and experimented with some of the techniques, you will be ready to tackle any wreath in this book.

One of the most exciting aspects of wreathmaking is the endless variety of possible design materials. While a quilter may be limited to

working with fabrics, and a cake decorator limited to confections, the only limitation a wreath designer must deal with is size, although one 36-foot vine wreath in the mountains of North Carolina tends to deny this idea. The seashells collected last summer with a special child are just as appropriate in a wreath as

traditional pine cones. The wine corks saved from special dinners can be arranged as creatively in a wreath as stems of dried flowers from last season's garden. Even perish-able items, such as the fresh radicchio and grapes used in

the centerpiece wreath on page 92 are fair game for wreath designers.

As you begin replicating a wreath from this book or working on your own design, keep in mind that it's almost impossible to make an ugly wreath. Inevitably, when you're halfway finished, you'll feel pangs of uncertainty that will make you want to stop. Don't. You'll soon be amazed at how many of the wreaths that seemed colorless, boring, or unattractive at the halfway point turn out to be cherished favorites after completion.

Once you're feeling secure in your wreathmaking abilities—and trust us, it won't be long—you may want to plan a wreathmaking party. The essentials are simple to assemble: a few wreath bases, some glue, picks and ribbon, a copy of this book, and plenty of good cheer. During the first part of December, invite friends over for hot cider and a memorable evening of creativity. Many fund-raising groups have enjoyed wreathmaking parties as a fun way to generate revenue.

Understandably, wreaths are increasing rapidly in popularity. While once relegated to the front door or over a mantel, they are now seen throughout the home in every room. They can be formal or fun, symbolic or silly, or just nice to look at. We celebrate this trend, and dedicate this book to everyone who enjoys this creative and fulfilling craft.

—*Dawn Cusick and Rob Pulleyn*

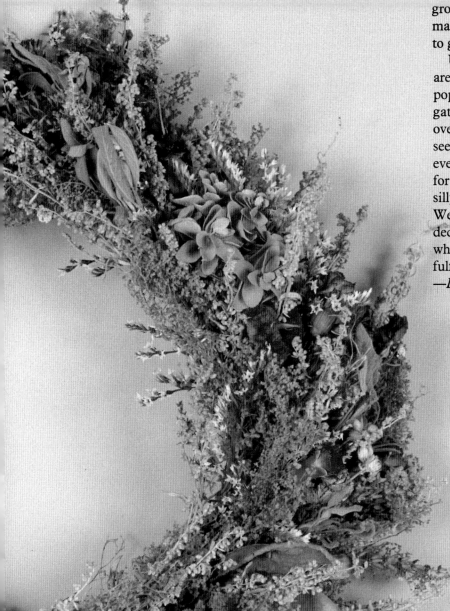

Bases

Twenty years ago most wreath designers had only a few types of bases to choose from. And while these bases (straw, moss, foam, and wire) are still popular, today's wreath designers enjoy a much larger and more creative selection.

Among the more creative options are foam bases with mirrors in the center, foam bases covered with grated cinnamon, bases made from floral foam to lengthen the life span of fresh flowers, and braided rattan bases in a variety of colors. This wide variety of materials (with corresponding variations in sizes and prices ranges) makes it a good idea to have a visual image of the type of wreath you'd like to make before you go shopping.

If you'll be covering the entire base with flowers or another design material, then it's okay to buy the most inexpensive base you can find. (If you'll be covering the base with unusually heavy items, though, look for foam bases that have been reinforced with wire.)

If you'll be allowing a portion of the base to show, then by all means choose a base that's visually compatible with your design materials and your home's decor. Moss, straw, and vine bases can also be highlighted with a light coat of spray-paint if desired.

Technical considerations for working with different types of bases are discussed on pages 12-15.

Making Your Own Bases

Making A Straw Base

To make a straw wreath base you will need several handfuls of straw, one coat hanger or length of heavy-gauged wire, and one spool (or several shorter lengths) of thin-gauged floral wire.

1) Begin by forming a circle with the heavy-gauged wire or coat hanger. You can approximate the size of the finished wreath relative to the size of the wire ring by adding the width of the circle to the width of the straw plus the width of the items you'll be decorating with. If your projected size comes out larger or smaller than you'd like, then adjust the size of the metal ring accordingly.

2) Next, gather small handfuls of straw and position them around the wire ring.

3) Holding the straw against the ring with one hand, use your other hand to wrap the thin-gauged wire around the straw and the ring at intervals of about one and one-half inches (four cm.).

4) Continue wrapping the wire until the entire base is secured. Trim the wire (after making a hook, if desired) and shape your base to a more perfect circle.

Making Vine Bases

If you have access to natural vines, you may prefer to make your own vine bases. Always work with freshly cut vine, which is less likely to split during the bending process than older vine.

When working with excep-tionally long vines: form a circle a little larger than the size you'd like your finished base to be. Continue adding rows of vine to the circle until you've reached the thickness desired. Secure by wrapping the vine horizontally around the base.

When working with vines of shorter lengths: hold four to six vines together and form a circle. Secure them together by overlapping the edges and wrapping a single piece of vine horizontally around the base.

Making Bases From Double-Wire Ring Forms

Available in craft supply stores, double-wire ring forms are made with a small groove that runs all the way around the circle and can be filled with any number of natural materials to create a custom-made base. Popular choices of materials include a variety of mosses, fragrant sweet Annie, and artemisia. Some of these materials, such as the mosses, can be packed into the groove when fresh and left to dry in place. Materials that shrink during the drying process (as most flowers and herbs do), though, should be dried first and then packed into the base.

1) Pack the groove with your selected material all the way around the base.

2) Secure the material in the base by tightly wrapping a length of quilting thread at two-inch (five-cm.) intervals around the base. Macrame thread and floral wire can be used instead of quilting thread. See pages 53-top and 83 for wreaths made with this type of base.

Preparing A Base For Three-Dimensional Arrangements

Creating full, three-dimensional arrangements is often a difficult task when working with ordinary wreath bases because there simply isn't enough surface area to attach the necessary number of items. The techniques described below reveal a florist's creative solution to this problem.

1) Cut a square or rectangular shape of floral foam to the desired size. Secure it to the base with wire and/or hot glue.

2) To prevent unsightly foam from showing in your completed wreath, cover the foam with moss, using floral pins. Then, pick or hot-glue your materials as you would with an ordinary foam base.

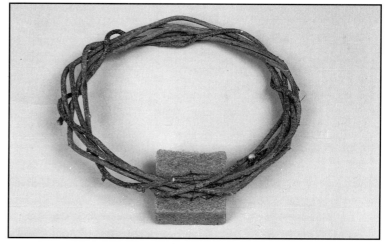

Glue Guns

For many people, glue guns are intimidating tools, something to avoid at all costs. If you're one of these people, take a quick look at the wreaths on pages 79, 90, and 99. They were assembled in a matter of minutes with a glue gun, and without one the time would have tripled.

Glue guns can secure such an incredible variety of items to a wreath base that after working with one for ten minutes you will find yourself considering design materials that you never would have before. For such a small investment (under ten dollars for smaller models), they are definitely worth purchasing. "Warm melt" glue guns are now available in most parts of the country. While the glue in these guns gets hot enough to melt, it does not get hot enough to cause severe burns.

Tips

• While your glue gun is heating up, spread a protective layer of newspaper over your work area. If your glue gun does not have a stand, find a glass plate or other non-flammable item to rest it on.

• You may notice strands of glue that resemble spider webs on your wreath. Don't worry about them as you're working—they'll easily pull off later.

• When working with foam, test a small surface of the foam to make sure the hot glue won't melt it. If melting does occur, use floral pins to cover the foam with moss and then glue the floral materials to the moss.

• Hold larger items in place for at least a minute after gluing to ensure proper bonding. Extremely large or heavy items may need to be attached with heavy-gauged wire and then hot-glued for reinforcement.

• Unplug your glue gun as soon as you've finished using it and never leave an unsupervised child near a glue gun.

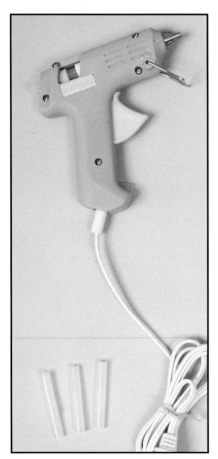

Application Order

Generally, the focal point of the wreath is attached first (usually because it's the largest in size), and smaller items are then arranged and hot-glued around it. A wreath's focal point can be anything from a large bow to a knick-knack to a bundle of greenery.

Attach items in their order of weight and delicacy, with the heavier items attached first and the lighter, more delicate items attached last. Hot glue can also be used to add smaller accents to picked wreaths. See pages 74 and 75 for examples.

Bases

Foam—although items can be hot-glued directly to foam, most designers do not because it's difficult to prevent bare areas of the foam from showing through in the finished wreath. Instead, they can be covered with moss or ribbon and then decorated.

Straw—items can be hot-glued directly to the straw or after it's been covered with moss or ribbon.

Vine—small items attach extremely well; larger items may need to be wired first and then reinforced with hot glue.

Floral Picks
and Wire

Floral Picks

Floral picks are a versatile tool for wreath designers. Although best known as a practical way to design with delicate flowers and greenery, picks make non-floral items, such as small bows and ribbon loops, easy to work with also.

Items without a stem or other vertical area to wire the pick to can also be picked by hot-gluing the flat end of the pick to the item and then inserting into the base as usual. Generally, floral picks are sold in inexpensive bunches. They can be purchased green, brown, or in their natural wood color. Choose the color that will blend best with the materials you'll be wiring. (Greenery, for instance, would obviously call for green picks.)

Picks should always be inserted into the base at an angle, and continue to be inserted at this same angle all the way around the base. Space your insertions so that each newly picked material fully covers the previous pick. If desired, cover the inner and outer rims in the same way.

Although picks can be used with almost any type of base, each one has its own distinct characteristics and challenges.

Straw bases have long been popular choices for picked wreaths of dried flowers. Commercially-made straw bases often come with a layer of green plastic around them, which some designers prefer to remove while others leave on.

Foam bases also work well with picks, although you may want to cover the foam with ribbon or moss before picking to prevent bare foam from showing through in your finished wreath.

Vine bases can also be picked. Bases with loose weaves may require placing a dab of hot glue on the end of each pick before insertion for extra stability.

How To Pick An Item

1) Hold the stem and the pick together, making sure there's enough stem to reach the top of the pick and that the flower (or other item) is above the wire.

2) Begin tightly wrapping the wire around the stem and the pick. At the point where the wire connects with the pick, make several extra turns with the wire.

3) Continue spiraling the wire down the stem until the wire ends. If desired, clip the stem at the end of the wire so the pick will perforate your base easier.

Picking Bunches

1) Arrange the items together as you would a small bouquet, and then follow the above directions.

Floral Wire

Knickknacks, novelties, and even large bouquets of silk greenery can be attached to a wreath base with floral wire. The only problem with wiring is that it's often difficult to find an inconspicuous place to wire the item, although solving this problem may provide inspiration for new designs. With a bouquet of silk greenery, for instance, you might cover the wire with small stems of dried flowers or plastic berries.

Although more than one type of wire will work, floral wire (available in craft supply stores) is often the easiest to work with. Floral wire comes in a variety of thicknesses (referred to as "gauges") and is inexpensively priced. Thin or medium gauges of wire usually work best. If you're wiring an unusually heavy item, though, you may want to consider using a heavy gauge. For extra support, the item can be wired to the base and then reinforced with a dab of hot glue.

Wiring works well with almost every type of base.

How To Wire An Item

1) Look for an area on your item where the wire will not show. (In the case of the rabbit shown below, the neck area was chosen because the bow will hide the wire.)

2) Wrap the wire around your item, positioning the wire so that both ends are on the back side of the item. Then tightly twist both ends of the wire together.

3) Choose the exact location on the base you'd like your item to appear. Holding the object tightly against the base, twist the wires together again until the tension is tight. Reinforce with hot glue if necessary.

Flowers

The natural beauty and abundance of flowers have made them a traditional favorite of wreath designers for hundreds of years, and 20th-century technology has significantly increased their versatility. The following descriptions should give you an idea of your choices, along with the strengths and limitations that apply to each.

Fresh—The short life span of fresh-picked flowers has deterred many wreathmakers from using them, but florists are now selling small plastic water tubes that extend a flower's display period by several days. The tubes attach easily to a wreath base with hot glue or wire, and new flowers can be inserted into them as the older flowers begin to wilt.

Drieds—Although dried flowers seem the perfect compromise between fresh flowers and those made by machine, many people—even avid gardeners—seem reluctant to dry their own flowers.

Drying flowers does not require special supplies or equipment, only a corner in a warm, dry room. While flowers can be picked at any time during their blooming cycle, be sure the moisture from a morning dew or rain shower has evaporated before picking. Then simply tie a cluster of flowers together at their stems with string or yarn and hang them upside down. Drying times will vary depending on the type of flower and the amount of moisture it contains, but you should check on its progress after two weeks.

Flowers can also be dried with moisture-absorbing substances (called "desiccants"), such as silica gel, borax, sand, and cat litter, although flowers dried with this method tend to re-absorb moisture when exposed to a damp environment.

Some flowers, including baby's breath, German statice and caspia, can be picked into a wreath base when fresh and left to dry in place. and a tremendous variety of dried flowers can also be found in craft supply and department stores.

Dried flower wreaths should not be displayed in direct sunlight (to prevent their colors from fading) or where they might be knocked into or brushed against (to prevent shattering).

Silks—Although most silk flowers are actually made from polyester blends, their manufacturers are increasingly attentive to the range of color and texture selections they're offering, with special emphasis placed on "hot" design colors.

The thin-gauged floral wire that usually lines the stems of silk flowers makes them easy to manipulate within an arrangement or around a wreath base. And while you may find the price of some silk flowers intimidating, keep in mind that an 18-inch (46-cm) stem can be trimmed down to five or six smaller stems. (Use wire cutters or old scissors for cutting.) Silk flowers are the ideal choice for outdoor wreaths.

Parchment Paper—Flowers made from parchment paper are an increasingly popular alternative to silks. Substantially more durable than their name implies, these flowers are often sold in bud form so designers can arrange the petals to appear in various stages of bloom. Their stems are also lined with thin-gauged floral wire. Parchment paper flowers are a good choice for wreaths that will hang in a damp, moist room, such as a bathroom or kitchen, because they will not re-absorb moisture and droop as some dried flowers will.

Seed Pods,
Seed Heads, and Cones

While pine cones have been a popular choice for holiday wreaths for a long time, many equally attractive natural materials—such as seed pods, seed heads, and other varieties of cones—have gone virtually unnoticed by wreath designers.

Many craft stores are now offering some very unique selections, although an attentive stroll through almost any wooded area is likely to yield an interesting variety of items. Many large, flowering trees, such as the magnolia, are also a good source for interesting seed heads and should be checked in the fall. (Tip: To prevent insect infestation, you may want to bake your collected items for 30 minutes in a 200° F (93° C) oven.

Since the natural colors and textures of seed pods, heads, and cones blend so well with wreaths made with ever-greens, herbs, and flowers, they'll usually need only a quick wipe with a damp cloth after harvesting before using. For more contemporary wreaths, though, you may

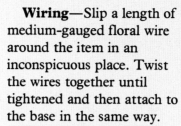

wish to add color with spray-paint. Metallic colors—gold, silver, and copper—seem to work especially well.

These materials can be attached to wreath bases in a variety of ways. For a more secure attachment, though, you might consider combining two of these methods.

Wiring—Slip a length of medium-gauged floral wire around the item in an inconspicuous place. Twist the wires together until tightened and then attach to the base in the same way.

Floral Picks—Hot-glue the flat end of a long floral pick to the item, and then pick into the base as usual.

Hot Glue—Trim the stem off at the base of the seed head or pod, then hot-glue directly to the wreath.

The seed pods and heads shown here include lotus pods, monkey pods, bell cups, mahogany pods, salignum, curly protea, coconut flowers, cortez flowers, and cedar base.

Ribbons and Bows

The perfect bow has the potential of being the highlight and personality of a wreath, often transforming an average wreath into an extraordinary one. Generally attached to a wreath base with a length of floral wire, bows can be easily changed with the seasons.

Since the selection of ribbons varies so widely in color (from hot pink to the palest pastels), in texture (from sensuous velvet to natural raffia), and in print patterns (from Victorian florals to modern plaids), some discerning shopping will almost certainly lead you to the perfect material. Following is a list of the more popular bow materials, along with some of their unique characteristics and a page reference so you can look at a sample.

Satin—an attractive material to cover foam bases with; available in a wide range of colors and sizes; not a good ribbon for beginners since it cannot be re-used; does not ship well; see page 30.

Cotton—good material for beginners to work with since crease marks can be removed with a hot iron; often creates a country mood; wider ribbon can be cut in half vertically if desired; see page 38-center.

Paper—ties easily into a variety of bows; provides interesting texture; holds its

shape well after tying; easily re-shaped if crushed; ribbon can be re-used again and again so it's ideal practice material for beginners; holds up well in outdoor wreaths; see page 55.

Velvet—adds a very formal, traditional look to a wreath; easily crushed and not re-usable; difficult for beginners to handle (especially difficult when the backing is plastic instead of satin); see page 39.

Cellophane—the metallic colors add a contemporary flair to a wreath; easy material for beginners to work with; can be re-used; does not fade in sunlight; see page 102.

French—the thin strips of wire lining the wrong side of this ribbon make it easy to work with; holds shape well so it's a good choice for wreaths that will be stored in an attic part of the year or shipped across the country; see page 35.

Lace—its soft, romantic look is ideal for wedding and anniversary wreaths; needs to be very stiff when purchased to hold its shape; unstiffened lace can be placed on top of a satin or cotton ribbon and tied with it; see page 99.

Raffia—its natural look and texture complement wreaths of natural materials; easy to work with; can be dyed to the color of your choice; see page 29.

Evergreens

From the days of early civilization when the Romans used evergreens to celebrate their holidays, to the beginnings of Christianity when evergreens were seen as a symbol of fertility, evergreens have been cherished and revered as a special gift from nature. Even today, evergreen wreaths are a popular way to decorate the home during cold winter months.

Evergreens come in all shapes and sizes, and in such a wide range of green hues that it's difficult to recognize these color differences unless you actually place a variety of clippings side by side. Many evergreens also emit that distinct fragrance that many of us associate with Christmas.

If evergreens will make up the background of your wreath, then the stems (if sturdy enough) can be cut at a sharp angle and inserted directly into the base. If evergreens will simply be an accent in your wreath, then the stems can be cut short and hot-glued in place.

Some evergreens, such as princess pine, boxwood, and ivy, can be used when fresh and allowed to dry naturally in the wreath. Another option is glycerin-preserving. Evergreens preserved in this manner are more supple than their naturally-dried counterparts, and will retain their green color for years to come.

To glycerin-preserve an evergreen, fill a small container with three parts water to one part glycerin.

Make several angular cuts in the evergreens' stems and stand them in the liquid. As time passes, the evergreens will absorb the glycerin mixture through their stems. The process usually takes about two weeks, but you should let the evergreens' appearance dictate the exact amount of time. Slight color changes are normal, with most evergreens darkening in hue.

Several common varieties of leaves also do well with glycerin-preserving, although their fleshier stems may necessitate a higher glycerin-to-water ratio. (See pages 41, top, and 48 for wreaths made from glycerin-preserved leaves.)

Evergreens can be glycerin-preserved in almost any type of container. Marking the liquid line with an ink pen will advise you of any water evaporation.

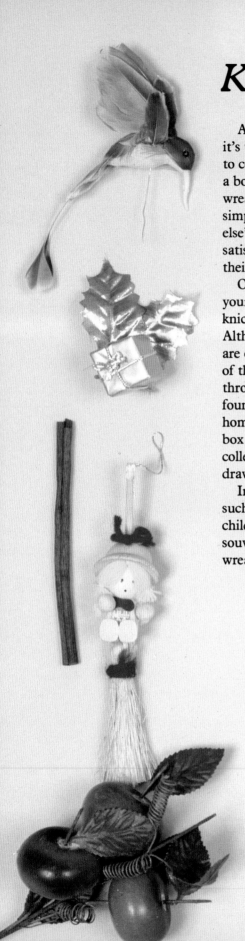

Knickknacks and Novelties

As you may already know, it's usually a simple process to copy a favorite wreath from a book or magazine. For many wreathmakers, through, simply replicating someone else's design is not very satisfying unless they add their own personal touches.

One easy way to personalize your wreaths is to add knickknacks and novelties. Although craft supply stores are often a good source, many of the items shown here and throughout this book were found around a designer's home, in an almost-forgotten box of memorabilia or collecting dust in a junk drawer.

Inexpensive keepsake items, such as gifts from small children and vacation souvenirs, add charm to a wreath and also serve as daily reminders of special memories. Other fun knickknacks and novelties include Christmas ornaments in all shapes and colors, party favors, silk fruits and vegetables, holiday decorations from around the year, sale items from your local five-and-dime, and children's toys.

Although securing these items to a wreath is usually quite simple, you should base which method you will choose on how permanent or transitory you can see the item's place in the wreath.

Hot Glue. Simple and quick, hot glue adheres to almost every surface, and allows items to be attached at unusual angles and directions. Novelties can be hot-glued directly to the base or to other materials that have already been secured to the base. (Tip: If your items are unusually heavy, they can be hot-glued to the flat end of a long floral pick and then inserted directly into the base. See pages 36 and 57 for examples.)

Wiring is also quick and simple, yet it allows items of sentimental and monetary value to be attached and removed from a wreath without damage. The challege with wiring, of course, is finding an unobtrusive place to wrap the wire. (See pages 72 and 106 for examples.) Extremely heavy items may need to be wired to the base first and then reinforced with hot glue.

Cleaning and Preserving Your Wreaths

While most wreaths will not last forever, a little extra care can lengthen their life span.

1) Exposure to sunlight and moisture may damage wreaths made with dried materials, so choose your hanging locations with care.

2) Wreaths made of delicate dried materials can be cleaned with the tip of a feather or a paint brush. Wreaths with sturdier dried materials can be given a light dusting using a hair dryer on its cold air setting. (Hold the dryer at least a foot away from your wreath.)

3) The sheen of glycerin-preserved materials can be restored by wiping them with a damp cloth.

4) When not in use, store your wreaths in loose paper bags in a dry location. (Plastic bags will cause condensation.)

5) Wreaths made from nuts and cones should be sprayed with a protective layer of polyurethane, shellac, or hairspray.

Winter Warmers

Canella berries, strawflowers, wormwood, German statice, and small myrtle (branches and berries) created the enticing combination of color and texture in this winter wreath.

All of the materials were naturally air-dried after harvesting and then picked into a double- wire ring base filled with silver king artemisia.

The base for this large
Christmas wreath was made
by stretching a 25-inch
(63-cm.) store-bought vine
base into an oval shape.

Next, a silk rose spray was
designed and attached with
wire. Dried caspia and
eucalyptus were wired in next,

and the outside of the wreath
was outlined with a copper
ribbon secured with hot glue.
Branches of silk ivy added
fullness to the arrangement.

As an extra touch, thin
pieces of looped and curled
copper wire were added to the
arrangement.

This holiday poinsettia wreath is at home in a country cabin or in a formal dining room.

Branches of glycerin-preserved cedar were first picked into a grape vine base to form the outline of the design. A large silk poinsettia was wired on next, with streamers of raffia picked under the flower.

Stems of dried gynestia, silver dollar eucalyptus, seed pods, and sweet Annie were then picked in around the cedar. As an extra touch, the designer highlighted the eucalyptus with gold spray-paint.

Tip: For extra strength, a small dab of hot glue was added to each floral pick before inserting it into the base.

Above

Cinnamon sticks, blue silk flowers, and a plaid bow all contribute to the country mood of this wreath.

The bow was first wired to one side of the vine base and its streamers were curved around the wreath and hot-glued in place. Sprigs of silk pine were then hot-glued around the bow and the blue flowers were arranged and hot-glued next. Last, short stems of dried baby's breath and artificial berries were added.

A second, smaller arrangement was created on the opposite side of the wreath with cinnamon sticks, pine, berries, and dried flowers.

Left

With the addition of Christmas ornaments and a large red bow, a year-round grape vine wreath of dried caspia, yarrow, eucalyptus, oak leaf hydrangea, German statice, and pine cones easily converted to a holiday wreath.

This small Christmas wreath makes the perfect holiday decoration for a bathroom or guest bedroom.

Two-inch (5-cm.) stems were cut from a 14-inch (36-cm.) length of artificial berries and hot-glued to the base. Stems of dried caspia were then hot-glued around the berries, and a red bow was hot-glued in last.

This wreath took less than half an hour to complete.

The traditional Christmas colors in this holiday wreath were created with dried sumac heads (red), glycerin-preserved spruce (green), pine cones (brown), sweet gum balls (brown), and reindeer moss (light green).

The background of the wreath was formed by hot-gluing spruce stems into the grape vine base. The sumac heads and pine cones were hot-glued in next, with the reindeer moss and sweet gum balls added as accents.

The metallic ribbon used to wrap a foam base for this
holiday wreath updates the traditional beauty of Flemish
coloring.

An assortment of coordinating paper flowers and plastic
berries were then arranged and attached to the top of the base
with hot glue and picks. A length of silk cord replaced the
traditional ribbon for a more delicate look.

Left

Artificial fruits and spruce branches in shades of blue, teal, and green helped achieve the verdigris finish of this wreath.

Branches of silk spruce were first picked into a 20-inch (52-cm.) wire-reinforced foam base and secured with hot glue.

The papier-mache angel was then hot-glued into the spruce, and the fruits were picked around the angel. Last, pine cones and a metallic cord were wired to the base.

Note: If you like, the fruits and pine cones can be spray-painted with highlights of gold or copper.

Below

The base for this contemporary holiday wreath was made with leftover scraps of chicken wire and a handful of wild vines and twigs. The chicken wire was shaped in a long tube and then brought together to form a circle. Twigs and vines were then woven through the wire.

After the base was finished, it was spray-painted white and decorated with glitter. The large silver bow was added last with floral wire.

A 20-inch (52-cm.) wire-reinforced foam ring served as the base for this magnificent della robbia wreath.

The outer rim of the wreath was outlined with silk magnolia and boxwood leaves. A large tapestry-print bow was then added at the top of the wreath. The silk flowers and fruits were arranged next, with the heaviest items attached first.

All of the fruits were attached to the base with hot glue, while the flowers were picked in. They included silk roses, camellias, pomegranates, apples, peaches, and grapes.

Unlike most of the wreaths in this book, the materials were inserted and hot-glued in two different directions. Starting at each side of the bow, the designer worked his way around until the two sides met at the bottom center.

Left

This illuminated holiday wreath used simple, inexpensive materials to create a special look.

Small holes were first punched in the back side of each cup, and the cups were hot-glued around a straw base.

The Christmas lights (one, two, or three, depending on the brightness desired) were then pushed into the hole of each cup. The excess cord was secured near the base by resting it on several half-inserted floral pins.

Last, the front of the wreath was covered with green moss and decorated with silk evergreens, flowers, ornaments, and a bow.

Left

A store bought artificial pine wreath was embellished with simple materials for a festive front door wreath.

The large bow was wired on first, while the silk foliage and berry sprays were hot-glued into the pine.

Below

While boxwood and red ribbon wreaths are traditional holiday favorites, the designer of this wreath added an elegant flair to the tradition by working his velvet ribbon deep into the boxwood stems.

The illusion of a full bow was created by folding eight-inch (20-cm.) lengths of ribbon in half, wiring them to wooden floral picks, and inserting them directly into the base.

The boxwood for this wreath was picked into a wire-reinforced foam base while it was still fresh, and it will dry in place for years of enjoyment.

Large glycerin-preserved protea leaves formed exotic curves when picked into a 14-inch (36-cm.) straw base. Small bouquets of dried baby's breath created a pleasant contrast in size and texture.

The baby's breath shown in this wreath was tinted to a light green. And while many craft stores sell tinted dried flowers, you can add color to flowers dried from your garden by simply applying a light coat of spray-paint or dipping them in a dye bath. (Be prepared to invest some time and materials for experimenting.)

Right, bottom

This wreath of wheat stalks and artificial berry clusters illustrates how beautiful a wreath of simple materials can be.

The wheat heads were first gathered in small bunches and then wired to a narrow grape vine base. The berries were added last with hot glue.

Stems of colorful dried flowers—roses, wild yarrow (dyed red), narcissus, gypsophilia, and eucalyptus—were picked into a base of silver king artemisia.

The base was made by securing handfuls of dried artemisia to a 25-inch (63-cm.) length of medium-gauged floral wire with fine macrame thread. At about the 18-inch (46-cm.) point, the ends were curved around to form a circle and tied together with more macrame thread. The heart shape was then gently formed by hand.

The traditional Christmas colors and fragrances in this wreath were created with fraser fir, sumac, pearly everlasting, lavender, nigella, Queen Anne's lace, German statice, lamb's ear, and mint picked into a 12-inch (30-cm.) straw base. Some of the smaller materials, such as the pearly everlasting, were picked as clusters, while the larger materials, such as the sumac, were picked as singles.

Spring Flings

This wreath of fresh spring flowers was creatively designed for lasting beauty.

Flowers that the designer knew would dry well were simply hot-glued directly to a vine base. These flowers included acacia, sea foam statice, genista, and galax leaves.

The flowers needing special care to dry— roses, tulips, and stars of Bethlehem— were inserted into water-filled tubes that were hot-glued to the base. Dried wood mushrooms and wild mosses were added for variety.

As time passed, the flowers in the tubes were replaced with fresher flowers, while the surrounding flowers had dried in place and become a permanent part of the wreath.

Below

The light, airy feel of this spring wreath was created by attaching the materials in a random fashion, instead of following a rigid, symmetrical design.

The base was made from grape vines and then spray-painted white, and all of the materials were attached with hot glue.

The materials included: dried roses, caspia, statice, freesia, sumac, mosses and glycerin-preserved boxwood and princess pine.

Opposite page, below

An oval base of grape vine helped create the tableau setting of this wreath.

The designer began by wiring a bow to the bottom of the wreath, and then wiring in large artificial branches of pine and blue spruce. Next, plastic berry clusters, dried baby's breath, and a small bird were hot-glued around the bow and greenery. The top arrangement was created in the same way.

The color scheme can easily be changed to match any room's decor.

Right

The light, wispy look of this dried flower wreath was created by packing handfuls of fragrant sweet Annie into a metal base and securing them with a length of medium-gauged floral wire.

Stems of sunset heather, Queen Anne's lace, straw-flowers, simplicity roses, silver king artemisia, sea statice, and oregano were then picked into the sweet Annie base.

Below

The porcelain look of this silk flower wreath was achieved by dipping the flowers in a porcelain setting agent, allowing them to dry, and then spraying them with a light layer of white paint.

The flowers were then picked into a 14-inch (36-cm.) wire-reinforced foam base, with silk greenery hot-glued around the outer rim.

Right

Silk spring flowers—crocus, tulips, iris, and pussy willows—were arranged in color groupings and picked into a 16-inch (51-cm.) foam base.

Designer Tip

Many beginning wreathmakers wonder how professionals manage to create wreaths which are so symmetrical and at the same time appear free-flowing.

The designer of the wreath below worked by mentally dividing the wreath base into three equal areas and then designing one section at a time. (If you look for the blue silk flowers and notice their spacing, you should be able to visualize how the designer worked.)

Although not a focal point of the finished wreath, note how the inner and outer edges were decorated with stems of silk pine.

The magnolia leaves covering this 16-inch (41-cm.) straw base form a contrasting background for delicate blossoms of pink dogwood.

The leaves, which had been preserved with glycerin, were wired to wooden picks and inserted into the base. (Note: Getting the leaves to lie flat while curving them around the base may take some extra time and maneuvering.) See pages 22 and 23 for directions on glycerin-preserving.

The bow was then wired to one side of the wreath and small sprigs of dried baby's breath were hot-glued into the loops of the bow. The dogwood blossoms were simply picked into the base between the leaves.

Delicate pussy willows and dried roses were combined for a simple yet elegant bedroom wreath.

Stems of pussy willows were first cut to four-inch (ten-cm.) lengths and then wired individually to a circular-shaped coat hanger. After the entire base was covered, additional pussy willow stems were hot-glued around the wreath to add fullness. (Note: Because the pussy willows are so delicate, you should expect some breakage as you are working, although the pieces can be hot-glued back on.)

The dried roses were added last with hot-glue.

Left

An oblong base of grape vine created a simple background for a spring bouquet of silk flowers.

Single daffodil stems were first wired to the base, with stems of lantana blooms and foliage wired in next.

Since the materials in this wreath do well outdoors, the wreath makes an ideal decoration for a porch or front door.

Below

The natural vibrancy of blooming forsythia trees inspired the designer of this Easter wreath.

Two small bunches of forsythia branches were first inserted into one side of a straw base (about eight inches, 20 cm. apart), curved in a circle, and inserted into the other side of the base. (Tip: If needed, a thin gauge of wire can be used to help keep the circular shape.)

The wreath base was then decorated with a bunny rabbit, plastic Easter eggs and candy, fresh daffodils, and lace ribbon, all attached with hot glue.

Right

A metal ring filled with sphagnum moss formed the natural background for a display of dried spring flowers.

The moss was secured in the ring with a length of medium-gauged floral wire; the flowers—chamomile, jonquils, Dutch iris, roses, daisies, goldenrod, dianthus, and gypsophilia—were picked into the moss. (Hot glue would also have worked.)

Below

A store-bought straw base was covered with dried pine needles to provide a more contrasting background to bright spring flowers. The pine needles were secured to the base with quilting thread.

The dried flowers—roses, statice, daisies, Dutch iris, carnations, lavender, oak leaf hydrangea, narcissus, nigella, lepto, Christmas ferns, goldenrod, cockscomb, poppy seed heads, and daffodils—were picked directly into the base.

Below

A base of wild grape vine decorated with reindeer and sphagnum moss contributed to the bouquet-like appeal of this wreath.

The dried flowers and herbs were picked into a small block of floral foam wired to the bottom right side of the wreath. The flowers included narcissus, daffodils, roses, salvia guaranitica, daisies, Dutch iris, annual mimosa, ambrosiana, and goldenrod.

The soft pastel colors in this dried flower wreath were created with German statice, dyed gypsophilia, dianthus, annual statice, wormwood, salvia persiana, wild roses, silver king artemisia, and lepto. All of the flowers were dried by hanging them upside down.

The flowers were secured to a wire ring base by wrapping fine jeweler's wire around stems of small flower clusters. Each new cluster of flowers was positioned to cover the stems of the previous cluster until the entire base was covered.

Summer Frolics

A store-bought base of glycerin-preserved princess pine provided a bright background for an assortment of colorful spring flowers.

After wiring the paper bow to the base, the dried flowers were simply hot-glued randomly into the pine. The flowers included zinnias, statice, roses, daffodils, caspia, baby's breath, and heather.

Stems of eucalyptus and tree ferns were also added.

Foam core can be used by wreathmakers in a variety of ways. Cut in a circular shape, it makes a good base for lightweight materials such as beads or feathers, and it's flat enough to fit in the narrow space between a storm door and an outside door.

For the wreath shown here, several holly leaves, a pair of birds, and a base were cut out of a large sheet of foam core. The birds and leaves were then lightly spray-painted black, with care taken to make sure the foam core dried completely between each coat of paint.

The birds and leaves were then hot-glued to the base, with a length of gold ribbon added to visually connect them. Small pieces of tinted green reindeer moss were also arranged and glued, and red plastic berries were added last.

This fragrant wreath of eucalyptus and seashells serves as a beautiful reminder of a special vacation.

Approximately 100 four-inch (ten-cm.) stems of eucalyptus were first attached to floral picks and inserted into a 14-inch (36-cm.) straw base. The flat ends of wooden floral picks were then dabbed with hot glue and placed inside a selection of seashells, leaving the tapered end of the floral pick free to insert into the base. (Tip: Remember to insert the seashells at the same angle as the eucalyptus.)

Stems of dried caspia and pussy willows were added last as accents.

The designer of this wreath chose a Victorian-inspired color scheme to complement the colors in her formal table setting. A 16-inch (41-cm.) straw base was first covered with a background of dried German statice picked in clusters. A 25-inch (63-cm.) length of satin ribbon was then woven loosely around the wreath, with hot glue used in select areas for reinforcement.

Finally, the wreath was filled out with stems of tinted, dried baby's breath, pepper grass, statice, and parchment paper flowers hot-glued in place. Note: When making a dining room wreath, you may want to save enough small dried flowers to decorate coordinating place cards or napkin rings.

Left

This summer garden wreath makes a decorative wall hanging both indoors or out, and requires minimal care.

The base was made by cutting a 20-inch (50-cm.) circle from plywood. Fine chicken wire was then molded over the front of the wood and stapled on the back side. The chicken wire was then packed with damp sphagnum moss that had been mixed with dirt.

The succulents were then planted into the moss, with the heavier ones wired in place to encourage rooting.

The plants included: hens and chicks, bird's foot ivy, ferns, and assorted succulents.

Below

Dried indigo spires, veronica, daisies, cockscomb, Christmas fern, goldenrod, roses, gypsophilia, dianthus, annual mimosa, and salvia farinacea were picked into a base of reindeer moss.

The base was made by packing fresh reindeer moss into a double-ring metal frame and securing it with twine. Tip: Store-bought reindeer moss tends to work better if first soaked in a bowl of water until it softens. Since reindeer moss wreaths are fragile, they should be hung in a location where they won't be disturbed.

Above

German statice, lamb's ear, yarrow, pearly everlasting, feverfew, tansy, baby's breath, and Queen Anne's lace form the subtle hues of gold, silver, and white in this 15-inch (39-cm.) wreath.

The wreath began with a 12-inch (30-cm.) straw base, and the flowers were attached with wooden picks. The outer edges of the base were outlined first with several inches of German statice; the more delicate flowers, such as the tansy and lamb's ear, were added next, with the remaining flowers and herbs filling in the bare spots.

Left

Vibrant strawflowers and purple statice add color to a base of golds, creams, and browns achieved with yarrow, santolina, goldenrod, artemisia, echinacea, lamb's ear, and German statice.

All of the flowers were dried by hanging them upside down in a dry room for several weeks. The flowers were then trimmed to four-inch (ten-cm.) stems and picked into a 12-inch (30-cm.) base.

A rattan wreath base and an assortment of silk flowers and greenery were combined to create this colorful front door wreath.

A two-inch square (5-cm.) of foam was first hot-glued to the inner rim of the base and covered with sheet moss.

The floral arrangement was then created by picking silk flowers and greenery into the foam. For a more dramatic design, a large silk poppy was hot-glued to the top of the wreath.

A powder-blue paper bow enhanced the arrangement of bright parchment paper flower blossoms and soft dried flowers on this wreath.

The paper bow was first attached to a 14-inch (36-cm.) moss base with floral wire. Stems of pussy willows and German statice were then hot-glued under the bow and down each side, with the pink blossoms added last.

The top bow was decorated with the same materials and its streamers were attached to the back of the wreath with floral pins.

A winter stroll in the woods yielded the collection
of vines and twigs for this creative wreath.

The twigs were first cut to similar lengths (about
three inches, seven cm.) and then wired in small
bunches to a wire ring base. The stems of each new
bunch were positioned over the wire from the previous
bunch and wired until the entire base was covered.

Short stems of dried flowers were then hot-
glued into the twigs. They included roses,
various colors of statice, pepper berries,
and pussy willows.

Above

The energizing contrast between vibrant reds and greens and neutral golds and creams in this wreath was created with dried ambrosiana, eucalyptus, caspia, German statice, wild yarrow, clover, poppy heads, and veronica.

All of the materials were picked into a 16-inch (41-cm.) straw base.

Left

Incredibly, most of the flowers for this natural wreath were found on the road side growing wild. After the flowers had been dried, they were picked into a rectangular piece of foam wired to the bottom of a wild grape vine base.

The flowers, herbs, and greenery included echinacea purpurea, Queen Anne's lace, wild yarrow, joe-pye weed, roses, veronica, oregano, pepper grass, and Christmas ferns.

Flexible artificial twig branches wired to a
heavy-gauge wire ring created the base for
this wreath of pastel paper flowers.

The heavier flowers were wired to the base
first, while the lighter ones were attached with
hot glue. The flowers incldued crocus, pussy
willows, narcissus, apple blossoms, and berries.

Last, small white ribbon loops were hot-
glued around the flowers.

Fall Harvests

The vibrant sunset colors in this 16-inch (41-cm.) wreath can be intensified or subdued by moving the wreath to a location with more or less light.

All of the flowers and herbs were harvested from a summer garden and dried by hanging them upside down from the rafters of a barn.

The flowers and herbs included bee balm, calendula, ironweed, santolina, statice, yarrow, celocia, nigella, and strawflowers; they were all picked into a straw base.

Below

This simple Halloween wreath makes a festive front door decoration to welcome trick-or-treaters.

Black and orange ribbons were first wrapped around a 14-inch (36-cm.) straw base and secured with corsage pins.

All of the materials were then picked into the straw base. When the holiday has passed, remove the novelties and ribbons and use the base for a new wreath.

Celebrating the vibrant colors of fall, this wreath makes an ideal gift for a leaf-lover living in a tropical climate.

Small handfuls of twisted Spanish moss were first hot-glued onto a base of willow branches. Glycerin-preserved oak leaves were then hot-glued to the moss, with stems of German statice and silk chestnuts hot-glued into the leaves as accents.

Long admired for its fragrance and color, eucalyptus also makes a versatile base.

For the wreath shown here, long branches of eucalyptus were cut into four-inch (ten-cm.) pieces and then wired individually to a base made from a circular-shaped coat hanger.

After the eucalyptus base was completed, cinnamon sticks, walnuts, almonds, dried caspia, and pyracantha berries were hot-glued into the eucalyptus.

This colorful harvest wreath incorporates craft novelties
and flowers into a background of glycerin-preserved boxwood.
The boxwood stems were first trimmed to four inches (ten
cm.) and wired individually to a circular-shaped coat hanger.
Cornhusk dolls, assorted paper flowers, dried caspia, roses,
sumac, salvia, and a small basket were then arranged around
the wreath and hot-glued in place.

Right

Roses, carnations, dianthus, and pepper berries added festive color to this wreath of dried herbs. All of the flowers and herbs were picked into a 16-inch (41-cm.) straw base.

The herbs included burnet, Mexican sage, basil, chamomile, dianthus, anise hyssop, wormwood, lavender, oregano, sweet woodruff, spearmint, peppermint, lemon balm, rosemary, feverfew, dill, and sweet majoram.

Below

Stems of dried artemisia, ironweed, lamb's ear, mint, sage, yarrow, Queen Anne's lace, and feverfew were picked into a 12-inch (30-cm.) straw base for a natural variety of color and texture.

Right

Vibrant silk and paper flowers were hot-glued to a 16-inch (41-cm.), moss-covered foam base.

Below

A thick vine base spray-painted with an autumn shade of copper created the warm mood that emanates from this festive wreath.

The shape of the arrangement was made first with stems of dried sable and silver dollar eucalyptus inserted with picks. The large sea grape leaves were added next, with dried roses and wheat stalks added last as accents. (Note: As shown here, dried leaves can be partially or completely covered with a light coat of spray-paint.)

For extra strength, add a small dab of hot glue to the tip of each floral pick before inserting it into the base.

78

Below

Natural mosses, dried flowers, and berries were hot-glued to an eight-inch (20-cm.) foam base to create a colorful kitchen wreath.

Small pieces of brown and green moss were first hot-glued around the base, alternating colors. Every other patch of brown moss was then covered with pepper berries, and the remaining brown patches were decorated with German statice, purple statice, and leptosporum.

This large, fragrant wreath serves as a showcase for an herbalist's summer and fall gardens. All of the herbs were picked into a 16-inch (41-cm.) straw base. Flowers and greenery were also added for variety.

The dried materials included seven varieties of sage, horehound, echinacea, chives, ivy, cayenne peppers, iris pods, yarrow, globe thistles, grasses, three varieties of heather, golden marguerite, anise hyssop, curry, two varieties of veronica, hydrangea, three varieties of bee balm, feverfew, bay leaves, elsholtzia, calendula, coreopsis, maple, three varieties of oregano, lavender, sweet Annie, goldenrod, four varieties of artemisia, sumac, geranium, garlic, lamb's ear, and rudbeckia.

Allowing a portion of the natural straw base to show enhances the harvest theme of this Thanksgiving wreath.

The base was first wrapped with ribbon (secured in the back with floral pins) and the bow was wired to the top.

Stems of glycerin-preserved ferns were then hot-glued on each side of the bow, and berry sprays were inserted with floral picks.

Last, short stems of dried baby's breath were hot-glued into the arrangement for a more natural look.

Celebrations

The base for this baby shower wreath was made by filling a double-wire frame with dried sweet Annie and securing it with a medium-gauged floral wire.

Stems of dried annual mimosa, anise hyssop, Dutch iris, dyed oak leaf hydrangea, indigo spires, and salvia guaranitica were picked into the base. Tip: The popular sweet Annie fragrance can be rejuvenated by gently rolling several blossoms between your fingers.

This children's party wreath adds excitement to any celebration.

A 12-inch (30-cm.) foam base was first wrapped with pink ribbon. Groups of ten-inch (25-cm.) lengths of ribbon were then clustered together, attached to floral picks, and inserted into the base. Festive curls were then added to the ribbons.

Small pieces of assorted candy were attached directly to the base with a small amount of hot glue, while the lollipops were inserted directly into the base with their sticks. (Note: Take care not to use too much hot glue or the candy will melt.)

A party wreath makes any birthday more festive, and using a foam base allows the wreath to be decorated with easily-removable party favors and treats.

First a long length of yellow ribbon was wrapped around a 16-inch (41-cm.) foam base. Colorful Hawaiian leis were then wrapped around the wreath and secured in the back with sewing pins. The large bow and bouquet of balloons were attached with wire, and the party favors were pinned around the base with corsage pins.

This charming wedding wreath was designed to hang on the outside of the church door during the ceremony and then become a fun part of the reception festivities.

A 16-inch (41-cm.) foam wreath base was first wrapped with 1¼-inch (three-cm.) white moiré ribbon secured on the back side of the base every three to four inches (seven to ten cm.) with white tipped dressmaker pins. The large bow was then wired to the top of the wreath, and the silk greenery and flowers were pinned to the base around each side of the bow. Small pieces of glycerin-preserved plumosa ferns were then hot-glued around the silk ivy for a more natural look.

The birdseed bags were made by placing a table-spoon of birdseed in the center of an eight-inch by four-inch (ten-cm. by 25-cm.) rectangular-cut piece of tulle, and tying it with white ribbon. The bags were attached to the wreath base with dressmaker pins, and small satin rosebuds were hot-glued to some of the bags for an extra touch.

While bridal wreaths are a beautiful part of any wedding, they also make lasting keepsakes of the special day.

For the wreaths shown here, a base was made by forming a loop with wire and then loosely covering the wire with pink or white tulle. Next, a bouquet holder (available from florists and many craft supply stores) was secured to the base with wire and filled with a flower arrangement.

If your bride will be using fresh flowers, be sure to buy a bouquet holder with oasis foam in it to increase the flowers' longevity. For the bride's wreath shown here, heather and caspia were chosen as the fresh flowers because they dry well and maintain most of their original color.

A 16-inch (41-cm.) foam wreath base with a mirrored center was a natural choice to reflect the beauty of fresh miniature carnations.

The life span of the flowers and fresh galax leaves was increased by inserting them into a small piece of oasis foam that had been hot-glued to the bottom of the wreath.

The base was then picked with silk greenery, berries, and evergreens. Ribbons, glass ornaments, and pussy willow branches were hot-glued last into the greenery.

Mirrored bases are equally attractive with simple designs. Stems of silk flowers and greenery were simply trimmed to four-inch (10-cm.) lengths and then inserted into the base.

This wreath makes a lovely gift for an anniversary or wedding.

While it won't last forever, the warm beauty of this fresh wreath makes it well worth the effort.

All of the materials were hot-glued to a 16-inch (41-cm.) base. They included silver dollar eucalyptus, acacia, safflower, wood mushrooms, moss, pin cushion protea, and grape bunches.

When the fresh items wilt, they remove easily, allowing the base to be reused for a new wreath.

Fresh and dried flowers were combined on a vine base for a special wreath centerpiece. Several water-filled tubes were first hot-glued to the base and then filled with orchids. The dried materials—mimosa, statice, moss, miniature carnations, and galax leaves—were then hot-glued around the water tubes.

Designer Tip

If you love to garden and enjoy making wreaths, floral tubes will become an indispensible tool for you. Available from craft stores and larger florists in several sizes, they can be wedged into a vine base for easy removal or hot-glued in place.

Simple, everyday materials often help create the most beautiful wreaths.

The wreath shown here was made from fresh radicchio and grapes to form a decorative centerpiece for a buffet table.

A ten-inch (25-cm.) straw base was first covered with overlapping radicchio leaves secured with floral pins. The grape bunches were then added to finish the look.

After the party, the base can be stripped and reused for a new wreath.

This small wreath of nuts makes a festive table decoration during the holidays.

The mixed nuts were first arranged and hot-glued around a small vine base, and a light coat of gold spray glitter was added last.

Since this wreath took less than half an hour to make and the materials were inexpensive, a morning's work could easily produce ten Christmas gifts.

After being admired for a respectable length of time, this chocolate wreath should be enjoyed to its fullest and eaten!

A small foam ring was first dipped in tempered chocolate and the tulip-shaped dessert cups were then attached to the base with melted chocolate.

While you could make this wreath at home, you might consider calling a local candy shop for assistance. (They usually have large vats of tempered chocolate that make covering the foam base a simple task for them.)

Designer Tip

Many dried flowers can be dyed or spray-painted to a variety of colors. To dye flowers, simply dip the flowers in a dye bath (prepared by following the directions on a box of powdered dye) and then hang them upside down to dry.

Flowers that dye well include yarrow, goldenrod, hydrangea, baby's breath, and pepper grass.

Dried yarrow, goldenrod, and hydrangea (tinted blue and green) were first hot-glued to a honeysuckle vine base.

Two potpourri-filled fabric hearts were then hot-glued in the middle of the flower arrangement to add color and fragrance.

Year 'Round Whimsies

An ordinary grape vine base decorated with simple materials created this whimsical tribute to nature. A store-bought bird's nest (available in craft supply stores) was first hot-glued to the base. The birds were then positioned and hot-glued in place and small clumps of Spanish moss were tucked into the vine. Last, a length of gold ribbon was hot-glued to a bird's beak, meandered through the vine, and then hot-glued to the other bird's beak.

Left

A summer of Saturday morning walks in the park yielded the collection of bird feathers used to create this large wreath.

The feathers were inserted directly into a 20-inch (50-cm.) foam base, with care taken to insert them all at the same angle.

To form the bow, ten-inch (25-cm.) clusters of copper ribbon were picked together, inserted into the base, and curled.

Because this wreath was made without hot glue, it makes an ideal children's project. Tip: If your feather supply is limited, be sure to choose a smaller base.

Below

A 20-inch (50-cm.) length of hand-braided raffia formed the base for this wreath centerpiece.

A small rectangle of foam was first wired to the base where the two ends of the raffia braid were joined. The foam was then covered with Spanish moss and secured with floral pins. The dried flowers were inserted into the moss-covered foam with floral picks.

The flowers included caspia, pepper berries, roses, and dyed sweet Annie.

Light spring flowers and grasses were arranged with miniature evergreen trees to create this magical winterland wreath tableau.

Six evergreen trees in varying sizes (available in craft supply and five-and-dime stores) were first wired and then hot-glued to the bed. Next, an arrangement of dried baby's breath, delphinium, honesty, hydrangea, lamb's ear, and wild grasses was hot-glued around the bottom half of the base.

As a final touch, small stems of baby's breath were hot-glued into the evergreen branches to create the illusion of snow.

A large bread basket served as the base for this country lace wreath.

The outer arrangement was created by hot-gluing a row of lace ribbon to the inner and outer perimeters and then filling the area in with dried German statice and tinted pepper grass. Small fabric hearts were then hot-glued around the wreath at the same angle as the flowers.

The inside arrangement was created by forming a heart with lace ribbon, hot-gluing it in place, and adding a bow in the center.

This wreath transformed a beachcomber's collection of driftwood into an unusual centerpiece.

The wreath began with a twig base that was wrapped with wild vines. Assorted sizes of driftwood were then arranged and hot-glued to the base, with dyed reindeer moss and parchment paper plants hot-glued around the driftwood.

Anything circular (or capable of being shaped into a circle) can serve as a base, as the barbed-wire base of this wreath demonstrates.

The arrangement was made by wiring a rectangular block of floral foam to the bottom of the wreath and covering it with moss. Two pieces of old fence wood were then arranged and hot-glued to the base. Dried flowers and seedpods were picked into the foam to form an arrangement.

A bolt of gold foil ribbon inspired the designer of this festive Christmas wreath.

The ribbon was first wrapped around a 16-inch (41-cm.) foam base and then secured at the beginning and the end with floral pins.

Stems of dried sea grape leaves, silver dollar eucalyptus, protea, sabel palm, bear grass, and euk fruit were then spray-painted gold and picked into the base.

This holiday wreath extends a festive welcome to a New Year's or Mardi Gras celebration.

The base was made with braided electric wire that was spray-painted copper, and all of the decorations were attached with floral wire.

(Note: Hot glue does not adhere well to this base's surface.)

Fun variations of this wreath can be created by adding bow ties, champagne bottles, wine glasses, or other festive novelties.

Fragrant kitchen wreaths are a fun way to display the bounty of a summer herb garden. After drying, the herbs were picked into a six-inch (15-cm.) base. They included mint, scented geranium, oregano, sage, sweet bay, yarrow, cayenne pappers, and garlic. Sumac and nigella were also included.

The Brazil nuts were added last by drilling small holes through the shells, threading a thin-gauged wire through the hole, and wiring it to the base. Hot glue would also work.

An afternoon walk in the woods yielded all of the materials for this large wreath.

The designer began by forming a base with heavy grape vine. The deer skull was then attached to the bottom of the base with a heavy-gauged floral wire and reinforced with hot glue. Last, rusty fence wire and mosses, lichen, tree branches, and wasp nests were arranged and hot-glued around the skull.

An ordinary wicker paper plate holder wired to a 16-inch (41-cm.) straw base created the focal point for this wreath celebrating special occasions throughout the year.

The base was first divided into 12 equal sections. Each section was then decorated with symbolic knickknacks using wire, floral picks, and hot glue.

Monthly calendars were then glued around the wreath and 12 small hooks were added to the back of the base so it could be turned each month.

Contributing Designers

A word of thanks goes out to all of the designers who worked on this book, each of whom generously contributed their time and creative energy.

Julianne Bronder studied at the American Floral Art School in Chicago. She now teaches floral design and does commissioned works. (Pages 31-top, 38-center, 41-top and bottom, 45-bottom, 48, 50, 57, 58, 65, 73, 82, 85, 86, 89, 99, 100.)

Corinne Erb has been designing with flowers for 17 years. She enjoys incorporating her experience in painting, weaving, and multi-media artwork into her floral designs. (Pages 44, 55, 74, 75, 93-top.)

Fred Tyson Gaylor taught art in the North Carolina public school system for ten years before changing careers to showroom and movie set design. He is currently a product designer for Hanfords, Inc., a wholesale holiday accessory company in Charlotte, North Carolina. (Pages 24, 33, 34, 36, 39, 46, 47, 66, 70.)

Cynthia Gillooly owns The Golden Cricket, a floral design studio in Asheville, North Carolina. She enjoys designing with innovative and natural materials. (Pages 19, 21, 29, 32-top, 43, 60, 78-bottom, 79-right, 84, 90, 91, 92, 97, 102, 112.)

Anthea Masters works as a display designer for Hanford's, a national wholesaler of gift lines. Anthea's love of old-fashioned English garden flowers is often reflected in her wreath designs. (Pages 6, 78-center, 94, 105.)

Claudette Mauter, owner of the Yellow Mountain Flower Farm, grows and dries all of the ingredients in her popular wreaths. (Pages 42, 62, 63, 71, 76, 80, 104.)

Nancy McCauley gathers and grows the natural materials for her wreaths and uses traditional drying and dyeing techniques. She markets her arrangements under the name of "From Gran's . . .", from her studio in Oak Ridge, Tennessee. (Pages 1, 5, 16, 27, 30, 32, 40, 45-top, 52, 53, 54, 61-right, 68, 69, 77, 83.)

The Sandy Mush Herb Nursery is the full-time passion of the Jayne family. They grow an extensive variety of herbs which they sell through their mail-order catalogs. (Pages 42, 62, 63, 71, 76, 80, 104.

Michael Staley and **Aubrey Gibson** operate the Gibson House, in Asheville, North Carolina, a floral decorating service catering specifically to weddings, parties, and banquets. They politely admit that their only two limitations in floral design are imagination and ceilings. (Pages 28, 38-left, 51, 56, 64, 72, 86-left, 87, 88, 103, 106.)

Also thanks to . . . Elizabeth Albrecht (Page 49); The Chocolate Fetish, Asheville, N.C. (Page 93-bottom); Joy Clay (Page 86); Judy Kidd (Pages 30, 83); Lowell McCauley; Micah Pulleyn (Pages 95, 98); Tim Sigmon (Page 101); Nicole Victoria (Page 22); Dawn Wade (Pages 96, 97); Tommy Wolffe (Page 35).

Common and Latin Names

Mexican sage . . . . *Salvia leucantha*
Mimosa . . . . *Mimosa*
Mint . . . . *Mentha*

N

Narcissus . . . . *Narcissus*
Nigella . . . . *Nigella damascena*

O

Oak . . . . *Quercus*
Oak leaf hydrangea . . . . *Hydrangea*
Orchid . . . . *Orchidaceae*
Oregano . . . . *Origanum pulchellum*

P

Pearly everlasting . . . . *Anaphalis*
Pepper grass . . . . *Brassica*
Peppermint . . . . *Mentha Xpiperita*
Pin cushion protea . . . . *Protea*
Poinsettia . . . . *Poinsettia pulcherrima*
Poppy . . . . *Stylophorum diphyllum*
Princess pine . . . . *Pipsissewa*
Protea . . . . *Proteaceae*
Pussy willow . . . . *Salix caprea*
Pyracantha . . . . *Pyracantha*

Q

Queen Anne's lace . . . . *Daucus carota*

R

Reindeer moss . . . . *Cladonia rangiferina*
Rosemary . . . . *Rosmarihus*
Rose . . . . *Rosa*

S

Safflower . . . . *Carthamus tinctorius*
Sage . . . . *Salvia officinalis*
Salvia . . . . *Salvia*
Salvia farinacea . . . . *Salvia farinacea*
Salvia persiana . . . . *Salvia persiana*
Santolina . . . . *Santolina*
Scented geranium . . . . *Pelargonium graveolens*
Sea grape . . . . *Ephedra distachya*

Sea foam statice (also known
as Sea statice) . . . *Limonium carolinianum*
Silver dollar eucalyptus . . . *Eucalyptus cinera*
Silver king artemisia . . . . *Artemisia albula*
Small myrtle . . . . *Myrtus communis*
Spanish moss . . . . *Tillandsia usneoides*
Spearmint . . . . *Mentha spicata*
Sphagnum moss . . . . *Sphagnum (sp.)*
Spruce . . . . *Picea*
Star of Bethlehem . . . . . . *Campanula isophylla*
Statice . . . . *Limonium*
Strawflower . . . . *Helichrysum*
Sumac . . . . *Rhus canadensis*
Sweet Annie . . . . *Artemisia annua*
Sweet bay . . . . *Laurus nobilis*
Sweet gum . . . . *Liquidambar styraciflua*
Sweet majoram . . . . *Origanum majorana*
Sweet woodruff . . . . *Galium odoratum*

T

Tansy . . . . *Tanacetum vulgare*
Ti tree . . . . *Cordyline terminalis*
Tulip . . . . *Tulipa*

V

Veronica . . . . *Veronica*

W

Wheat . . . . *Triticum*
Willow . . . . *Salix*
Wormwood . . . . *Artemisia*

Y

Yarrow . . . . *Achillea*

Index

Bibliography

Mauter, Claudette and Pulleyn, Rob
    Everlasting Floral Gifts.
    New York City, New York: Sterling Publishing, 1990.

Pulleyn, Rob
    The Wreath Book.
    New York City, New York: Sterling Publishing, 1988.